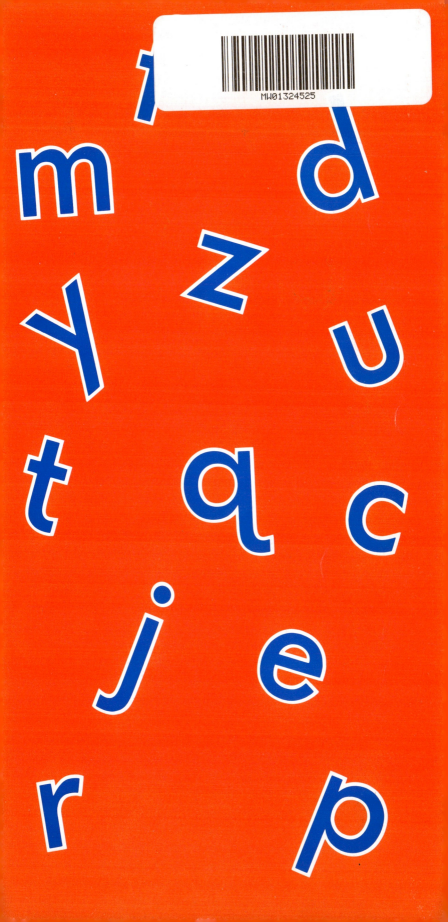

The National Gallery

abc

Children's Universe

a

apple

b
baby

C

cat

d

dog

elephant

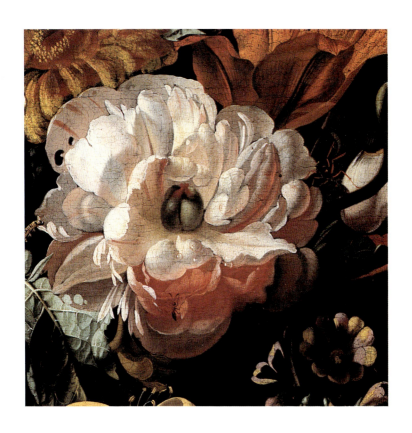

f

flower

g
girl

h
hands

i
insect

k
kiss

l

m

mouse

nest

orange

p
parrot

q
queen

r

rabbit

s

snail

tiger

U
umbrella

W
windmill

y
yacht

z

zigzag

Index of Paintings

a
Altarpiece: The Annunciation,
with Saint Emidius
Carlo Crivelli active 1430s to 1494?

b
Adoration of the Shepherds
Bernardino da Asola recorded 1526

c
A Woman and a Fish-pedlar
Willem van Mieris 1662–1747

d
Bathers at Asnières
Georges Seurat 1859–1891

e
Orpheus
Roelandt Savery 1576–1639

f
Flowers in a Vase
Rachel Ruysch 1664–1750

g
The Graham Children
William Hogarth 1697–1764

h
Christina of Denmark,
Duchess of Milan
Hans Holbein the Younger 1497/98–1543

i
Fruit and Flowers in a Terracotta Vase
Jan van Os 1744–1808

j
Marriage à La Mode:
The Suicide of the Countess
William Hogarth 1697–1764

k
Charlemagne, and the Meeting of Saints
Joachim and Anne at the Golden Gate
Studio of the Master of Moulins
active 1483 or earlier to about 1500

l
Saint Jerome in a Landscape
Bono da Ferrara active 1442(?) to 1461(?)

m

Fruit, Flowers and a Fish
Jan van Os 1744–1808

n

Flowers in a Terracotta Vase
Jan van Huysum 1682–1749

o

Still Life with Oranges
and Walnuts
Luis Meléndez 1716–1780

p

Lady Cockburn and her
Three Eldest Sons
Sir Joshua Reynolds 1723–1792

q

Dido receiving Aeneas and Cupid
disguised as Ascanius
Francesco Solimena 1657–1747

r

The Agony in the Garden
Andrea Mantegna
about 1430/31–1506

s

Still Life
Attributed to
David Davidsz. de Heem
active 1668

t

**Tropical Storm with a Tiger
(Surpris!)**
Henri Rousseau 1844–1910

v

Children making Music
Jan Molenaer about 1610–1668

u

The Umbrellas
Pierre-Auguste Renoir 1841–1919

x

The Umbrellas (X-ray)
Pierre-Auguste Renoir 1841–1919

w

A Windmill by a River
Jan van Goyen 1596–1656

y
Boats pulling out to a
Yacht in a Calm
Willem van de Velde the Younger
1633–1707

z
Altarpiece: The Virgin and Child
with Saints Jerome and Dominic
(Predella)
Filippino Lippi 1457(?)–1504

First published in the United States of America in 1994
by UNIVERSE PUBLISHING
300 Park Avenue South
New York, NY 10010

© National Gallery Publications Ltd 1994

All rights reserved. No part of this
publication may be reproduced, stored in a
retrieval system, or transmitted in any
form or by any means, electronic, mechanical,
photocopying, recording, or otherwise, without prior
consent of the publishers.

94 95 96 97 98 99 / 10 9 8 7 6 5 4 3 2 1

Designed by Rowan Seymour
Printed and bound in Great Britain by
Cambus Litho Ltd, East Kilbride

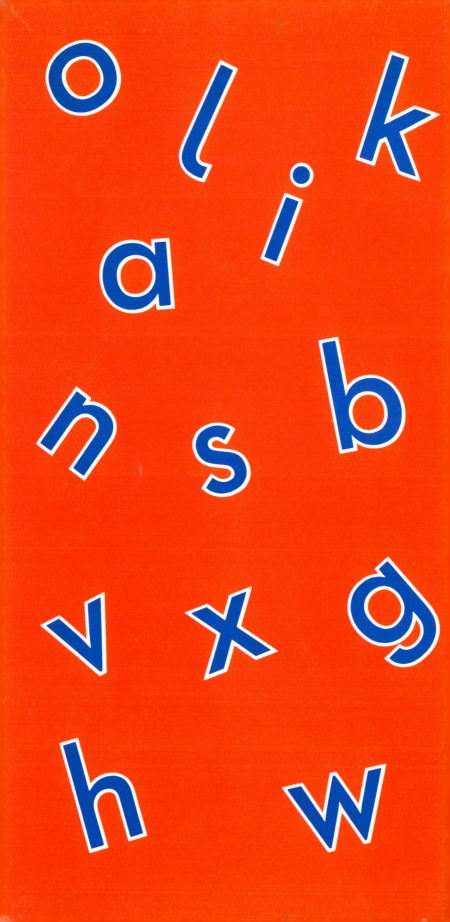